Table of Contents

Introduction 5

Chapter 1. What is SketchNoting? 7

Chapter 2. Why Is SketchNoting So Effective? 8

Chapter 3. Benefits of SketchNoting 10

Chapter 4. What Do I Need to Get Started? 14

Chapter 5. Basic Elements of SketchNotes 18

Chapter 6. A Step-by-Step Guide on The Effective Use of SketchNote and SketchNoting 23

Final Words 28

Thank You Page 30

Sketchnote Workbook For Beginners: Easy and Effective Techniques of Taking Visual Notes to Simplify and Organize Your Work and Business

By Dale Blake

© Copyright 2014 Dale Blake

Reproduction or translation of any part of this work beyond that permitted by section 107 or 108 of the 1976 United States Copyright Act without permission of the copyright owner is unlawful. Requests for permission or further information should be addressed to the author.

This publication is designed to provide accurate and authoritative information in regard to the subject matter covered. This work is sold with the understanding that the publisher is not engaged in rendering legal, accounting, or other professional services. If legal advice or other expert assistance is required, the services of a competent professional person should be sought.

First Published, 2014

Printed in the United States of America

Sketchnote Workbook For Beginners:

Easy and Effective Techniques of Taking Visual Notes to Simplify and Organize Your Work and Business

By

Dale Blake

Introduction

As a child, you understood the amazing power of drawing and doodling and how it unlocked your imagination and creativity. For hours on end, you would lay in your room, sit at the kitchen table or sprawl out on the living room floor surrounded by crayons, markers and pencils drawing an endless array of figures and shapes in a variety of colors. Through doodling you could enter a world where anything was possible and everything that you could think and dream made sense.

As you got older, doodling was looked upon as being lazy and inattentive. Throughout junior high and high school, you would sit bored in science or social studies class filling your pages of your spiral notebook with sketches and assorted doodles that were mixed in with random lecture notes. As your went through your college years and into your career, you sat in countless lecture halls and conference rooms staring at PowerPoint presentations and listening to monotonous presentations, trying to find ways to be engaged and inspired.

As you sit down and take notes during business meetings and other presentations, you wish for a system in which you can take notes in a dynamic fashion. You want to be able to take plain, boring old notes and transform them into a medium that will give those ideas structure, clarity, meaning....and life. From these ideas, this innovative system of note taking can spur your creativity and you can be able to explore new creative avenues and come up with groundbreaking ideas that will take your business and career to new levels. You may wonder if a dynamic system of note taking exists, and it does—welcome to the world of SketchNoting.

Chapter 1. What is SketchNoting?

In its simplest and most pure form, the concept of SketchNoting involves taking what a speaker is saying or what is being said in a lecture or presentation, and creating a form of a visual story that will help you relate to those concepts in a highly personal way that will be easily remembered and integrated in your thought processes. Through the use of big uppercase letters, highlighting, color, squiggles, shapes and lines, you can create your own form of language that can take the oftentimes boring medium of presentations and make those experiences opportunities to uncover new ways of thinking.

The concept of SketchNoting was created by Wisconsin-based graphic designer Mike Rhode. Rhode used his experience as both a graphic designer and a print designer to create the SketchNoting form of notation. Through the use of SketchNotes, Rhode's ultimate goal is to help people unlock their creativity and visual thinking skills in order to understand ideas more clearly as well as be able to generate the communicate their own ideas.

Chapter 2. Why Is SketchNoting So Effective?

As you can conclude from the material in this book so far, SketchNoting is a form of visual note taking. In order to understand how the SketchNoting approach is taking the concept of visual note taking to a new level you must understand the ways in which note taking can be utilized. The first and most obvious method of note taking is simply writing down what is said and done during a meeting or lecture. Another method of visual note taking involves the use of visual notes that are provided by the lecturer or facilitator of the lecture or meeting. This facilitator is creating the notes as they go and will add new notes and points of emphasis which can spark new conversation and new avenues of thought.

While these methods of visual note taking can be effective in certain applications, these notes and ideas generally have more meaning to its creators than it would for you. This is where the concept of SketchNoting takes shape. SketchNoting allows you to connect thoughts, concepts and ideas together by using your own visual language. Research as shown that being able to visually represent content into a form of language that you can easily understand will help you not only retain those ideas and concepts, it can also help hone your visual thinking skills to create new concepts and ideas.

SketchNoting is an excellent example of what is known as the *dual coding theory*. The theory, which was first introduced in the early 1970's, states that the verbal processing and non-verbal processing systems in our brain functioning use different coding systems in order encode our verbal and memory experiences. While these two systems are completely different, they do find ways to interconnect and create deeper meaning. This is done through taking those external experiences (such as lectures and presentations) and stimulating the senses to create memory traces. These memory traces can be represented as figures, shapes and colors, all of which have deeper personal meaning and can be used to tie concepts together.

Chapter 3. Benefits of SketchNoting

Besides the active engagement in thinking skills and creativity in order to make presentation material have deeper understanding and meaning, SketchNoting has great benefits to those who engage in its practice:

You Don't Need to Know How to Draw

The first and best feature about SketchNoting is the fact that you don't need to have unbelievable drawing ability or experience. Even if you can barely draw a stick figure, once you grasp some of the basic forms, shapes and icons of the SketchNote "language" you can personalize it to fit your personality and learning style. Once you do more and more SketchNoting, you actually become better at drawing and after a while you become less conscious of what you are drawing.

You Can SketchNote in Real Time or After the Fact

SketchNoting can be adaptable to whatever type of learning and retention style that works best for the individual. For some people, they may be able to learn concepts and critically think about those concepts as a lecture or presentation progresses. While it can be difficult, it is possible to capture facts and ideas and be able to represent them in the moment. For others, they may want to revisit the information afterwards in order to let those facts and images settle in. In those instances, people can SketchNote in a rough and abbreviated form then be able to revisit that information and edit the information so it becomes more understandable and clear.

You Can Practice SketchNoting Anywhere

As with the acquisition of any new skill, SketchNoting takes practice to become more proficient as well as efficient. You don't have to wait until your next presentation to hone your SketchNoting skills. You can SketchNote your favorite sitcom, your daily schedule, your shopping list….the sky is the limit. Once you start SketchNoting during these activities, there may be other opportunities where you can hone these skills.

If you work in a certain field where symbols and shapes are common, utilize those in your SketchNoting and practice them over and over so they become engrained. Another great technique in building your SketchNoting skills is by listening to one thing while writing or drawing another thing.

No Worries about Editing

The concept of SketchNoting doesn't require the need for continual editing as you go. There is no need to capture presentations or lectures verbatim; you are able to paraphrase where needed so a concept is clear to you. You can also use quotes if you need to write down a direct quote. Additionally, if you lose your train of thought or feel that you are hitting a wall, you can simply take a break and rejoin the presentation or lecture when you mentally hit the rest button.

There are Many Resources to Help You

Do you feel stuck? Do you need tips on how to make your SketchNoting more efficient? In addition to the books that were written by SketchNotes creator Mike Rhode, there are many blogs and forums online that can provide you with tips and suggestions on essential SketchNote concepts. You can also go to YouTube and watch demonstrations of various SketchNote techniques.

You Can Create Notes that Everyone Will Read

Creating your notes through the SketchNotes method goes beyond other basic forms of visual and non-visual note taking methods. You are creating lively and engaging illustrations and storyboards of lectures and presentations that anyone would want to look at and be inspired. Whether it is a business presentation or college lecture, SketchNotes can make the mundane more exciting and make the tedious task of note taking an engaging and fun-filled activity.

Chapter 4. What Do I Need to Get Started?

So now you are ready to start your SketchNote journey and are ready to transform your mundane and linear-based notes into something engaging and exciting. To get started, you need to obtain a few supplies that will adequately do the job for you.

Paper

The absolute basics are a sketchbook and a decent pen. While you get start with a regular spiral notebook or regular lined notebook paper, the ideal medium to create your SketchNotes is on plain white paper that doesn't feature any lines, graphs or guides of any kind. You can start with regular typewriter paper, but obtaining a sketch book that contains 8 1/2'" by 11" paper is ideal. Sketchbooks can be cumbersome (especially if you are carrying other items), but the pages are thick and large and it can fold flat to lay on your lap. If you don't want to buy a sketchbook straight away, you can use a clipboard that holds single sheets of paper or an inexpensive notebook with a couple hundred pages. Additionally, you can use a smaller sketchbook or scrap paper if you wish.

Pens

For the purpose of SketchNotes, a black felt tip pen is perfectly acceptable as long as it is of good quality and won't run out of ink halfway through the presentation. In the event that your pen ink runs dry, always carry several pens in your bag and have them ready on the desk or table. While a pen with a 0.5 diameter is sufficient, you can experiment with pens with different diameters.

Highlighters

The use of different colored markers can be effective in SketchNoting for added depth and emphasis for specific words, phrases and can add frames and shading to any visuals that you draw. Ideally, you want to use thin-tipped markers that don't bleed through the pages. An example of a common highlighter that can be used in SketchNotes is a dual brush pen. This thin colored pens act works like a paintbrush and can deftly add color and fine lines to your text or drawings.

Correction Fluid

If mistakes are made in the process of note taking, having some correction fluid on hand is advisable. The inclusion of correction fluid is seen in some circles as being somewhat controversial since some believe that making mistakes helps with the learning process. However, if the mistake is minor and you are going to be presenting your SketchNotes to a friend of colleague it can be acceptable.

Booklights

For situations in which you are in lecture halls and conference rooms that dim lights, having a small, clip-on booklight is a great accessory to have. You simply clip in on to the edge of your sketchbook, notebook or clipboard so you can clearly see your paper for easier writing and sketching.

Tablets and Smartphones

Your Smartphone and Tablet can be a useful tool in the SketchNote process. You can use these devices to take pictures of your SketchNotes once they are completed. Not only do they provide a visual record of what you created, but you can send them to friends, colleagues and you can post them on social media sites such as Facebook and Twitter. Additionally, the photos will serve as a quality backup to your SketchNotes in the event your original copies are lost or destroyed.

For tablet or smartphone users or for those who prefer to take notes on laptops or notebooks, there are Sketchbook apps that are available for purchase. Apple offers a SketchNote app that can be purchased and downloaded from iTunes. With this app, you are able to write notes, free hand drawings and well as move and delete drawings. You are also able to create files using PDF and text formats. Similar apps such as Adobe Ideas, Flipink, SketchbookX, and ProCreate are also options you can explore if you are looking to SketchNote on a mobile device or laptop. You will need to carefully research applicable applications to find one that will best suit your needs.

Chapter 5. Basic Elements of SketchNotes

There are some basic design elements that are commonly used when people SketchNote that gives the finished product clarity and organization. It is important to understand and master these basic design concepts.

Handwriting

In the SketchNote style of handwriting, there are two different writing styles: *hand lettering and hand writing.* Hand lettering is usually large and bold and is often used for titles of presentations and is used to emphasize key words or phrases in a way that is visually stimulating. Hand writing is used for the writing of quick notes, complete sentences and is used to write phrases where speed and clarity are needed. Both of these styles give a sense of hierarchy in your note taking.

Titles

Titles are great to defining your SketchNotes and can include the name of the presenter, the place where the presentation took place, date, location and the topic of the presentation. You have the option of creating the same "template" for every presentation or you can change it up for every presentation. It is important to create your title before you start note taking.

Typography

The width, height and style of the way you write your notes help convey meanings. You can write in open block letters, employ more calligraphy-style penmanship, or employ other types of creative devices to make words come alive. For instance, if you write the word *nervous*, you can write the word with wavy or shaky lines to convey the uneasiness of the mood. Another example is the word *epic*. You can write that specific word using bold, block letters and surround it with rays of light, lightning bolts or even exclamation points.

Diagrams and Drawings

No matter what your skill level in drawing or doodling, you can create a quick illustration or a simple graph to help simplify concepts that are more complex. During your practice, a rudimentary exercise is the continual drawing of basic shapes such as circles, squares and triangles and basic objects such as houses, fish, clouds and trees. You can also use logos like Apple or Google if you wish. The symbols and shapes you use can be anything you want. Using diagrams and drawings can also help in explaining a process or tell a short story.

Dividers

The use of dividers in SketchNotes are to separate ideas from each other visually. You can create any kind of divider by using straight lines, dotted lines, separate dots and dashes, numbers, letters or other design elements.

Arrows

The use of arrows help you focus attention to certain phrases, words, procedures or diagrams. Arrows are also useful to help you and those who read your notes make connections between multiple ideas, diagrams and graphs.

Bullets

Bullets are useful when you need to delineate a set of ideas or if you need to highlight a single idea from a series of drawings or diagrams. You can use different types of bullet point styles to differentiate different sets of ideas. You can use periods, asterisks, stars, open circles or can employ any design.

Icons

If you have a repeating idea, phrase or motif that runs throughout your notes, you can use an icon to mark those repeating elements. Like bullet points, you can use any type of icon as long as you stay consistent in its application to a specific idea. If there are many recurring ideas or motifs that repeat, you need to use different icons to set them apart.

Containers

These SketchNote design elements help connect various themes or elements together to represent a common idea or overriding theme. Examples of containers include "thought bubbles", circles, squares or rectangles and enclose a word or a series of words that are joined together by lines or arrows.

Signatures

You can use a signature to identify your SketchNotes. While it is not required if you are just created notes for yourself, it can be utilized if you are sharing them with classmates, friends or colleagues. Having a signature is also helpful if your notes are being file shared or placed on social media sites. You can use your name, your Twitter identifier (@johndoe123 as an example) and you can add a simple doodle to make it more personal.

Framework

Most importantly, you need to consider what type of framework you want to utilize to organize the flow of your SketchNotes. You can employ a variety of different styles and can use a framework that best suits you and is easy for you to follow. You can choose a basic vertical framework in which information is presented from top to bottom, or you call follow a basic linear framework in which information is created left to right. If you want to be more creative, you can utilize a radial framework in which you have a central idea in the center of the page and have subpoints radiating outward. You can also adopt modular or even random types of framework.

Chapter 6. A Step-by-Step Guide on The Effective Use of SketchNote and SketchNoting

So you have your materials, know the basic elements of SketchNotes and have hopefully practiced these elements. When you are ready to SketchNote your first presentation or lecture, there is a basic step-by-step guide that you can follow to make the process easier for you.

1. *Research Your Topic*—before you go to any presentation, and especially one in which the topic is unfamiliar, you need to do as much research on that topic so you at least have some familiarity when you walk onsite. Research prior to the presentation also gives you confidence so you are able to take notes more freely and without significant pauses. You can bring research that you have printed from home or you can bring your smartphone or iPad to quickly research on the fly.

2. *Gather the Necessary Materials*—you want to be as completely prepared as possible before you come to a presentation. Bring a couple of sketchbooks, several

pens and your smartphone or iPad. It is also good to bring a small clip-on booklight in case the room is dim. It is always important to bring backups of everything.

3. *Get There in Plenty of Time*—you always want to come early to a presentation so you can scan the room to find the best possible seat. The ideal places that you want to sit are those areas where there is good lighting and the sight lines allow you clearly see and hear the presenter. You should try to find seating at or near the front row and always want to try and find seating in the middle of those rows. Sitting in the middle will allow you minimum distractions in the event that people are coming or going.

4. *Get Settled and Get to Work*—once you find your seat and get settled, open your sketchbook and create the title of the presentation. You want to include the actual title of the presentation, the speaker, date and time. You want to be sure you use the correct spelling of the speaker. You can use your smartphone to look up and find photos of the speaker for reference and to draw a visual of that speaker if you wish. By completing the title before the presentation, you are able to focus on the material itself and curating as you

go as opposed to rushing and disrupting your flow and train of thought.

5. *Start SketchNoting*—once the presentation starts, go with the flow and curate the content that you are seeing and hearing. It is important not to get bogged down with notating every word; you should try and summarize chunks of information as you go to make note taking easier. With the knowledge of basic principles and prior practice, the ability to SketchNote should be relatively easy. It is also important to use a circular mindset of actively listening, synthesizing the information and writing or sketching it in your sketchbook.

You should train your brain to store temporary ideas so you able to summarize those ideas and points concisely in your sketchbook. If you are constantly looking down at your sketchbook while the presentation is going on, you may miss important inflections or cues that may help you remember things later when you are revised and reviewing. As stated earlier, it is essential that you practice drawing common shapes and symbols thoroughly so when you actually start the practice of SketchNoting, you are able to keep with the flow of the presentation with minimal interruptions. If for some reason you lose your train of thought, or if you hit a wall and draw a blank, just simply rest your brain for a few moments and regroup. Once you are ready, you can resume taking notes.

6. *Take Photographs*—once your notes are complete, it is important to take pictures with your smartphone. As stated earlier, taking quality photos of your pages are an excellent way to share what you have created on social media sites such as Facebook or Twitter. You will also have the added benefit of having backup documentation if something happens to the original notes. Ideally, you want to try and shoot each page of your SketchNotes as single image. Taking pictures in this fashion will make your notes easier to view on your phone.

7. *Scan and Share*—once you get home, review and revise your SketchNotes. If you have a scanner, you want to scan the pages with as high a resolution as possible. You want to be sure to fix and typos or other errors before saving the document. Once it is finalized

and formatted, you are able to share your SketchNotes online with anybody anywhere.

An Added Benefit of SketchNotes….

If you have created a presentation using the SketchNote method, you can use them to promote an upcoming event because of their eye-catching visuals and overall presentation. Increasingly, organizers and presenters are giving our SketchNotes as PDF documents. These documents can be an excellent resource to review after an event as concluded.

Final Words

The SketchNote method of note taking is a highly visual and interactive system in which you take the information presented in lectures and other presentations and turn them into highly visual and engaging content in which you are the creator. While other method of note taking is often linear, lacking spark and is the vision of other creators, the SketchNote system of note taking allows you to take information and add doodles, sketches, symbols and different types of typography to create information that flows as your mind flows and using a visual language that facilitates deeper meaning.

The style of SketchNotes that you create can comes from many different templates and styles, which can be found in print and on the Internet. Mix and match print styles and format and don't be afraid to develop your own personality. The great thing about taking notes with the SketchNote method is that you are able to see yourself evolve over time. You can look back at your first attempts and see the progression in ideas and you are able to come up with better, more creative and more efficient ways to SketchNote in the future. Ultimately, SketchNotes are meant to be shared so you can see how people think, react and conceptualize. You can share your SketchNotes on social media, YouTube, through a personal blog, on Tumblr or you can email your creations to the official SketchNote Army website.

No matter how you create a SketchNote or how you share it, a SketchNote is a wonderful and highly personal way to thank a presenter for their presentation.

Thank You Page

I want to personally thank you for reading my book. I hope you found information in this book useful and I would be very grateful if you could leave your honest review about this book. I certainly want to thank you in advance for doing this.

www.ingramcontent.com/pod-product-compliance
Lightning Source LLC
LaVergne TN
LVHW021747060526
838200LV00052B/3524